© 1998
Published by Grange Communications Ltd
Edinburgh

Printed in the UK

ISBN 0 947782 21 4

CONTENTS

WHEN THREE BECAME ONE...

ALTHOUGH organised football had made its first appearance in the 'Granite City' as far back as 1881, it was a further twenty-two years before the club we now know and love as 'the Dons' was finally founded.

That came about when the original *Aberdeen Football Club* amalgamated with two of the other top sides in the area, Orion and Victoria United.

By that time, Aberdeen had moved to Pittodrie ('Dung Hill' in Gaelic!), having played at a variety of venues in the city namely, the Links, Hayton, Holburn cricket ground and the Chanonry. Orion meanwhile, popularly known as the 'Stripes', were based at Cattofield with United ('The Blues') opting for Central Park.

The red of today was still a long way off, with the original side's nickname of 'The Whites' giving away the colours of the day, this coming after a spell in maroon.

The reason for the merger between the three was quite simply in order to pool resources in an attempt to gain admission to the now established Scottish League, although a successful application was by no means guaranteed. Thus the present *Aberdeen Football Club* was officially formed on 14th April, 1903.

Unfortunately, Aberdeen's initial bid for Scottish League First Division status failed when, at the League A.G.M. in May, with two new places up for grabs, Motherwell and Airdrie were voted in ahead of the 'Dandies'. Such was the optimism in the Aberdeen camp, nobody had bothered to apply for the Second Division as a safeguard!

Thus the new *AFC*, with Jimmy Philip at the helm, had to make do with a place in the regional Northern League, a 1-1 Pittodrie draw with Stenhousemuir being the low-key inaugural match. Early results were hardly inspiring, with the Dons finishing third in the league behind Montrose and Arbroath and suffering a first-round Scottish Cup exit at the hands of Alloa.

Undeterred, a fresh application was made to both the First and Second Divisions of the Scottish League in time for the 1904 AGM and this time there was partial success, with acceptance into the lower tier, where Abercorn, Albion Rovers, Arthurlie, Ayr United, Clyde, East Stirling, Falkirk, Hamilton Accies, Leith Athletic, Raith Rovers and St. Bernard would provide the opposition.

Coinciding with Aberdeen's entrance to the 'big time' was the discarding of the white playing kit in favour of a new black and gold outfit, a colour scheme which was to remain for more than thirty years. Aberdeen's first-ever Scottish League clash resulted in a 2-1 'home' defeat by Falkirk, an outcome which set the tone for a disappointing league campaign, which saw the Pittodrie side finish seventh in the table.

However, whilst the team's league form was disappointing, there was cup success in the shape of the Qualifying Cup when, on 26th November, 1904, Renton were dispatched 2-0 in the Dens Park final. For the record, the victorious line-up that day was:- Macfarlane, Murray, D. McNicol, Halkett, Strang, Low, Robertson, G. McNicol, Lowe, McAuley, Ritchie.

Despite their modest displays in the league, the board of directors decided to again go for First Division status. It proved to be a case of third time lucky and on 22nd May, 1905, along with Falkirk, Aberdeen were elected to become part of an increased top flight, comprising sixteen teams, to participate in season 1905-06.

In preparation for doing battle at the higher level, several new players were brought in, notably ex-Queen's Park, Dundee, Rangers and Fulham winger, Willie Lennie, who was destined to become the first of many Pittodrie stars to be capped for Scotland.

Again Aberdeen started the season with a 'home' fixture, with Partick Thistle providing the opposition, and again, there was disappointment, with the 'Jags' triumphing by a single goal. The home side on that historic occasion of 19th August, 1905, read: Macfarlane, Murray, Brebner, Halkett, Strang, Low, Robertson, Henderson, Ward, McAuley, Lennie.

A fortnight later saw the Dons beat Kilmarnock 2-0 to register their opening First Division win and although the season was again something of a letdown in terms of results (twelfth out of sixteen), the men from the North-east had shown they could survive at this hitherto untried level.

One of the best signings made by Jimmy Philip in these early days was Irish international inside-left, Charlie O'Hagan, who arrived from Middlesbrough in late 1906 to form, with Willie Lennie, one of the best, if not *the* best, left-wing partnerships ever seen at the club.

Jimmy Philip

The next three seasons were ones of consolidation for the 'Black and Golds' before a best-ever finish of fourth place was achieved in 1909-10. At the conclusion of that season, Charlie O'Hagan was one of several key players to move on to pastures new and observers of the day were almost unanimous in concluding that the Pittodrie side would immediately return to the lower regions of the table.

In fact, the opposite was true and the following season saw Aberdeen mount their first genuine Championship challenge. Between the sticks was Arthur King, with Donald Colman, who, incidentally, invented the trainer's dugout, Jock Hume, George Wilson, Jock Wylie and James Miller providing a formidable defence. The width of the team, which caused opposing rearguards no end of problems, was supplied by Jimmy Soye, on the right, and Willie Lennie, with new signings, Pat Travers and Angus McIntosh also playing their part.

By late September, and having recorded their first win ever at Ibrox, Aberdeen had moved to the top of the table, a challenge which was maintained until late March - early April, when a poor run saw five points dropped in the space of four games. In the end, Aberdeen had to settle for the runners-up spot, finishing four points behind Rangers.

At the end of the 1910-11 campaign, history was made when Aberdeen embarked on their first-ever foreign tour, playing a total of eight games, seven of which were won, in the space of a fortnight.

The transfer of Pat Travers to Celtic prior to the new campaign did not please the Pittodrie 'faithful' one bit and matters were not helped when the player helped his new side eliminate the Dons from the Scottish Cup for the third year on the trot. In the league, Aberdeen slipped back, finishing eighth, although there was a small crumb of comfort when Donald Colman and Jimmy Soye were selected to play for the Scottish League.

Arthur King

Things grew even bleaker the following season when a shock first round Scottish Cup exit at the hands of Dumbarton, coupled with an extremely harsh winter, placed real financial pressure on the club. Consequently, wing-half Stewart Davidson, was transferred to Middlesbrough with 'keeper Arthur King going to 'Spurs', Third Lanark snapping up the versatile Willie Milne and Willie Lennie going to Falkirk for the princely sum of thirty pounds. It wasn't all one-way traffic, though, and in a bold move, popular 'stopper', Jock Wylie, who had moved south to Bradford at the end of the previous season, was persuaded to return to Pittodrie by manager Philip.

The exodus of players from the club went down like a lead balloon with the supporters and season 1913-14 saw Aberdeen finish in a lowly thirteenth position. However, as the Dons prepared to get their 1914-15 campaign underway and with their finances still in a poor shape, a far greater threat, not only to the equilibrium of the club, but to humanity itself emerged, when the world was plunged into war and with it, the organised chaos that was wartime football.

TWO WORLD WARS...
BUT NO TROPHIES

THE SCOTTISH football authorities thought long and hard before deciding to carry on as normal during the Great War. Whilst in some quarters the idea of continuing to participate in any sport was unthinkable in the circumstances, officialdom gave the Scottish Football Association their blessing to carry on as best they could, although the Scottish Cup was suspended for the duration of hostilities.

In the early stages, things did continue much as before, although Aberdeen's remoteness compared to the majority of the clubs in Scotland, coupled with an increasing drain on resources, affecting players and supporters alike, soon began to take its toll.

The backbone of the pre-war team comprising Donald Colman, 'Dod' Brewster, Jock Hume and Jock Wylie, along with Geordie 'keeper George Anderson, saw the Dons fulfil their commitments up to the end of the 1916-17 season, by which time the situation had become farcical.

At the end of that season, it was sensibly agreed that Aberdeen would withdraw from all senior competitions, a decision echoed by Dundee and Raith Rovers and one which stood until the commencement of the 1919-20 season, following the declaration of peace in November, 1918.

Many of those re-signed by the Dons after the cessation of hostilities were familiar to the Aberdeen support, although a Lanarkshire lad by the name of Jock Hutton, the first new player to come to Pittodrie after the war, was destined to become one of the North-east's most favourite adopted sons ever!

Conservatively estimated at weighing in around the fifteen stone mark, Jock, who had been spotted starring for Hall Russell's during the war, began his Dons career as an inside forward before being moved to fullback, a position in which he also distinguished himself wearing the dark blue of Scotland.

League football returned to Pittodrie on 16th August, 1919, when a healthy attendance of 9,000 witnessed a two-goal victory against Albion Rovers. That first season after the break was notable for a couple of points. The 25,000 who packed into the stadium for the 1-0 defeat by Celtic in November set a new record, as did the £1500 received from Everton for the services of Dod Brewster.

The close season of 1920 witnessed the end of an era with long established stars Donald Colman (now forty-two!) Jock Hume and Jock Wylie all moving on. There were also changes in the boardroom with chairman Tom Duncan stepping down after fourteen years to be replaced by William Philip, namesake of manager Jimmy.

The record transfer fee mentioned above lasted until May, 1922 when wing half Alex Wright joined Hearts for a fee of £2500. At the conclusion of the 1922-23 season, trainer Peter Simpson decided to call it a day with former star Pat Travers taking over.

Season 1922-23 also provided Aberdeen with their biggest win in the senior game, a scoreline that still stands and, frankly, is unlikely to be bettered. The date was the 10th February, 1923, the occasion the 3rd round of the Scottish Cup and the opposition, neighbours Peterhead.

Even before the match the Highland League team did not have their problems to seek with a wrangle over cash (nothing changes!) resulting in no less than eight of their normal squad refusing to play . . . the remainder must have wished they had joined their colleagues' protest!

In atrocious conditions and in front of 3,241 hardy souls, the Dons went in five goals to the good at the break and by the end had amassed a baker's dozen without reply against their luckless opponents! As if to emphasise the farce of the situation, home 'keeper Harry Blackwell donned a waterproof coat and for most of the ninety minutes sheltered under an umbrella borrowed from a spectator!

Turning out for the Dons on that momentous afternoon (goals in brackets) were Blackwell, Hutton, Forsyth, MacLachlan, Milne (3) Robertson Middleton (1) Thomson (4) Grant (3) Rankin (1) Smith (1). Unfortunately that game seemed to use up the Dons' goal allowance for the tournament and they were promptly dumped out of the competition by Hibs in the next round!

A poor 1923-24 season, despite another Cup semi-final reversal, ended with a tour of Germany, after which manager Jimmy Philip announced he was retiring, after guiding the Pittodrie club through its first twenty- one years. His successor was none other than Pat Travers, the former player who had taken over as trainer two years previously.

The new manager's first signings were two brothers from Dunbartonshire, Alec and Walter Jackson and when news of their signing was announced, nobody could have predicted that the former would go on to become one of the greatest players this country has ever produced! That, incidentally, brought the number of first-team regulars with the surname 'Jackson' to three, centre half Jimmy Jackson having signed from Motherwell the previous season.

Manager Travers was extremely busy on the transfer front in his early days at Pittodrie. Jock McHale was the next to arrive and then, just to add to the confusion, a fourth 'Jackson' arrived, in the shape of Willie or 'Stonewall', as he was affectionately called.

The 'Jackson Four' only lasted until the end of that season, with Alex, who had been a shining light in an otherwise dismal campaign, moving south to Huddersfield for a new club record of £4500. The tall winger then, of course, went on to gain football immortality with his 'hat-trick' for the 'Wembley Wizards' in 1928.

Pat Travers used some of the cash received from Huddersfield to purchase players such as Alec Reid from Third Lanark and Bob McDermid from Rangers, both of whom were ever-presents throughout the 1926-27 league programme, which ended with the Dons in eleventh position. Once again Aberdeen enjoyed a good run in the Scottish Cup and once again it finished with defeat at the penultimate stage.

Both the following two seasons saw Aberdeen finish in seventh place, as Pat Travers sought to mould a team capable of making a concerted bid for honours and in 1929-30, the Dons at last mounted a title challenge of real note.

Between the sticks was Duncan Yuill, who had taken over from the veteran Harry Blackwell and the defence contained promising youngster, Willie Cooper, and former

Benny Yorston

Cowdenbeath man, Jimmy Black, who had been playing football in the United States prior to being brought back home by Pat Travers.

Up front, there was an exciting blend of youth and experience including at centre-forward, a man who, for many was the greatest-ever 'Don', Benny Yorston.

As early as January 1930, Yorston had set a new scoring record for the Dons, beating the previous twenty-four netted by John Miller in 1921-22 and by the end of the season his tally had climbed to thirty-eight. Although they set the pace for much of the season, the Dons fell away somewhat in the latter stages before finishing a very respectable third.

Another indifferent twelve months followed before, in November 1931, undoubtedly one of the strangest stories to ever emanate from within Pittodrie broke into the public domain, creating rumour and counter rumour.

'The Great Mystery', as it came to be known, centred around the announcement from Pat Travers that five of his first-team regulars, Jimmy Black, David Galloway, Frank Hill, Hugh McLaren and Benny Yorston, would never play for the first team again.

Whilst no reason was ever given for this drastic action, Travers was as good as his word and all five played out their time at Pittodrie in the reserves before moving on to new clubs. To this day, no light has been shed on what the players had done which was so wrong, although several suggestions have been mooted, including a betting scandal, corruption and bribery! At various times after the announcement, the five each protested their innocence of anything corrupt but none would go further than that. And with almost seventy years having now elapsed, the background to what was at the time, the most sensational of stories, is unlikely ever to be known.

Despite the loss of so many regulars at the one time, Aberdeen ended the season in a creditable seventh position and over the next three years the side finished in a respectable sixth, fifth, sixth. In that last season, 1934-35, a first Scottish Cup Final looked on the cards after a 3-1 quarter-final Pittodrie victory against Celtic, in which Matt Armstrong, with two converted penalties, and Willie Mills, were on target.

However, semi-final opponents Hamilton Accies had other ideas and the Dons lost a keenly contested match 2-1, with Mills again the man who mattered. The cup jinx had struck again!

Season 1935-36 saw Aberdeen mount a real challenge in the league, with one of the chief reasons for the upturn in form widely accepted as being the fact that the normal eleven picked itself and, barring injury, read:- Smith, Cooper, McGill, Fraser, Falloon, Thomson, Benyon, McKenzie, Armstrong, Mills, Lang.

The Dons completed their league campaign for the loss of a mere three games and pushed both halves of the 'Old Firm' all the way in the process. At the end of the day, though, they had to settle for third place behind Celtic (who had a better 'goal average') and champions, Rangers.

The following season saw little change in the Dons team, with South African, Billy Strauss, replacing Johnny Lang at left wing the only alteration. An unbeaten run of eleven games from the start of the season was finally halted when Celtic won by the odd goal in five at Parkhead on 3rd October, although successive 'away' defeats at the hands of Third Lanark and Motherwell, in early 1937, virtually ended the Dons title hopes and they had to make do with the runners-up spot.

However, in the Scottish Cup, it looked as though, at long last, it might well be the Dons' year! Comfortable wins over Inverness Thistle and Third Lanark were followed by a 2-1 quarter-final success at Hamilton, in which Matt Armstrong and Billy Strauss were the scorers.

The same pair worked their magic in the last four, when Morton were dispatched 2-0 at Easter Road. The cup semi-final hoodoo had finally ended and Aberdeen were ninety minutes

Billy Stauss and his wife.

away from their first ever Scottish Cup, with Celtic standing between them and glory.

Unfortunately, Strauss, who had picked up an injury in the Morton match, had to sit out the final, with Johnny Lang stepping in for the game which took place on 24th April, 1937. The Aberdeen team was:- Johnstone, Cooper, Temple, Dunlop, Falloon, Thomson, Benyon, McKenzie, Armstrong, Mills, Lang.

In front of an incredible crowd numbering 146,433, Celtic took a tenth-minute lead through Johnny Crum, an advantage which lasted less than sixty seconds, with Matt Armstrong turning home Jackie Benyon's low cross. It stayed that way until after the interval, when Willie Buchan, much to the despair of the huge travelling support from the North-east, scored what proved to be the winner, although Dons defenders were insistent that Jimmy McGrory had knocked the ball on with his hand.

The goal stood and manager Travers and his players were again left to reflect on what might have been - the Dons were fast becoming the 'nearly men' of Scottish football.

As some consolation for their disappointment, the Dons had a summer tour of South Africa to look forward to. It proved, though, to be a trip which would be remembered for all the wrong reasons, namely the tragic death of Welsh wing wizard Jackie Benyon, due to peritonitis in a Johannesburg hospital. The loss of their teammate, just a few short weeks after he had made their Cup Final goal, hit the Aberdeen squad hard and the journey back to Scotland could not come soon enough.

In November 1937, Pat Travers decided to call it a day after thirteen years in charge at Pittodrie, moving to Clyde, where, ironically, within two years he was to win the Scottish Cup. One of his first signings at Shawfield was defender, Eddie Falloon, from his former team.

Aberdeen v Celtic, 1937.

The man charged with the task of replacing Travers was, somewhat surprisingly, former Dundee, Arsenal and Manchester City forward Dave Halliday, whose managerial experience was limited to stints at Yeovil and Petters United.

Halliday, who took over in early 1938, had only been at the helm for a matter of weeks when star forward, Willie Mills, left to join English top side Huddersfield Town. A reasonable league campaign ended with the Dons in sixth place, whilst the cup finalists of the year before were knocked out in a third-round replay at home to East Fife.

History was made in March 1939 when the Dons dispensed with the black and gold colours they had worn for more than three decades in favour of a simplified scheme of red shirts and white shorts.

The new manager was just beginning to make his presence felt (season 1938-39 saw the side finish third in the league and reach the cup semi final) when, for the second time in the club's history, matters of far greater importance took centre stage with the outbreak of

World War II in September 1939.

For the next seven seasons, the Scottish League and the Scottish Cup competitions were suspended, although the Dons did continue to be represented through a variety of more localised events including the Wartime League (East), North-Eastern League, Southern League, Mitchell Trophy, North Eastern Supplementary Cup, Victory Cup and Dewar Shield.

With most of the Aberdeen squad of the day serving their country outwith the area, the Dons were able to field basically anyone they wanted, including servicemen stationed in the locality. Thus such names as the great Stan Mortensen, who was to score a 'hat-trick' for Blackpool in the 'Matthews' FA Cup Final of 1953 turned out at Pittodrie, as did Sammy Cox (Rangers), Joe Harvey (Bradford), Ernie Waldron (Crystal Palace), George Green (Huddersfield) and Alex Dyer (Plymouth Argyle), to name but a few.

'Normal service' resumed at the beginning of season 1946-47, by which time *Aberdeen Football Club* was now forty-three years old and still looking for its first major trophy!

POST WAR AUSTERITY...
BUT ONLY OFF THE FIELD

SEASON 1945-46 was already underway when peace was declared and, as such, is recorded as 'wartime football', although the Southern League Cup, which produced one of the first big post-war dates on the football calendar, did not begin until February 1946.

Aberdeen, with Dave Halliday having returned to the helm, came through their section, which also included Kilmarnock, Hibs and Partick Thistle, to be rewarded with a quarter-final tie against Ayr United, which was duly won 2-0 at Dens Park. Airdrie were then dispatched, albeit following a replay, and the Dons were through to a Hampden final meeting with Rangers.

Prior to the clash on 11th May (a date which would take on even greater significance almost forty years later!), the Aberdeen FC party stayed at the Marine Hotel in Largs, where they spent three relaxing days preparing for what was going to be a major occasion.

The Aberdeen side, featuring three survivors from the pre-war Hampden line-up, read:- Johnstone, Cooper, McKenna, Cowie, Dunlop, Taylor, Kiddie, Hamilton, Williams, Baird, McCall and a massive crowd of 135,000 filled the national stadium for the occasion.

For the vast numbers of those present wearing red and white, it proved to be a dream start for the Pittodrie side, with a goal inside the opening minute. South African, Stan Williams, who had been spotted by the Dons in their 1937 tour to the country, was the man on target after good work from Andy Cowie and Archie Baird.

Amazingly, the Dons then went two up before the game was twenty minutes old, Williams again doing the damage, with Alec Kiddie, who enjoyed a tremendous afternoon, and George Hamilton involved in the lead up.

Aberdeen held their two-goal advantage until four minutes after the restart when Duncanson pulled one back. When Thornton levelled with twenty minutes remaining, the game looked to be swaying the Light Blues' way. However, with time running out and a replay looking on the cards, the Dons mounted one final attack.

Kiddie's cross was met by George Taylor, who gave Shaw in the 'Gers goal no chance whatsoever - at long last, the Dons were winners at Hampden! The victory also heralded the start of what was to prove to be one of the best periods in the Pittodrie club's history.

'Normal service' resumed at the commencement of the 1946-47 term and it was one in which the Dons got themselves off to an absolute flyer, being the early league pacesetters before being overtaken by Rangers, who eventually lifted the title, with the Dons finishing third.

In the cup competitions Aberdeen dazzled, reaching Hampden twice in the space of a fortnight! The League Cup had now been established as the country's third major tournament and the Dons had battled through their section which featured Falkirk, Queen of the South and Motherwell, before ending the hopes of Dundee and Hearts to set up a 5th April, 1947 meeting with Rangers at the national stadium.

Unfortunately, the final turned out to be a one-sided affair, with the Dons capitulating by four goals without reply. However, just fourteen days later they returned to the same venue, this time to face Hibs at the last stage of the Scottish Cup.

The road to Hampden had been a momentous one. In the opening round, 34,000 had packed into Pittodrie for the visit of Partick Thistle, who were defeated 2-1, the winner being a 40-yard 'wonder strike' from veteran fullback, Willie Cooper.

Round two saw Aberdeen enjoy a Pittodrie eightsome reel at the expense of poor Ayr United, in which George Hamilton and Tony Harris both notched trebles, ably assisted by strikes from Stan Williams and Ray Botha. It took a replay to ease past Morton in the third round, a 2-1 success at Cappielow being the outcome following a 1-1 draw, before Dundee were beaten 2-1 in one of the first games to feature a 'golden goal' or 'sudden death' extra time, as it was called then.

The semi final against Arbroath, which was contested at Dens Park, actually took place a week after the Dons League Cup Final reversal and just seven days before the final itself! Just imagine the reaction of the clubs if such a programme was suggested these days!

A Stan Willams brace ended the hopes of the Angus outfit, although some of the shine was taken off the victory when Willie Cooper pulled a muscle, an injury which ruled him out of what would have been his last chance to win a Scottish Cup medal, after giving twenty-one

Aberdeen 2 Hibs 1, 1947.

years of distinguished service.

Hibs, who featured future Dons manager, Eddie Turnbull, in their side, were Aberdeen's opponents in the 19th April final, with the Pittodrie team as follows:- Johnstone, McKenna, Taylor, McLaughlin, Dunlop, Waddell, Harris, Hamilton, Williams, Baird, McCall.

A second Hampden disaster within a fortnight looked very much on the cards when John Cuthbertson, taking advantage of an uncharacteristic gaffe from George Johnstone, put the Edinburgh side in front after only a minute's play.

With almost the whole game still to play, there was plenty of time for the Dons to respond and after weathering the storm, they hit back in the thirty-sixth minute with a fine header from George Hamilton. Six minutes later, Aberdeen were in the driving seat, thanks to one of the cheekiest goals ever witnessed in a cup final.

A Tony Harris pass seemed to be going out of play until Stan Williams caught it, to the right of the Hibs goals. With Hamilton and Archie Baird screaming for a cross and the Hibs defence preparing for exactly that, the little South African spotted a slight gap between 'keeper Jimmy Kerr and his left hand post. The angle was such an acute one that, nine times out of ten, the shot would have missed its target. However, on this occasion, from a Dons perspective, it was simply perfect and Kerr and his fellow defenders looked on in horror as the ball nestled in the back of the net.

It proved to be the decisive strike, although Hamilton scorned a great opportunity to put the issue beyond doubt when he saw a second-half spot-kick saved by Kerr. The Dons had lifted the Scottish Cup for the first time in their history!

There were amazing post-match scenes as the huge Dons contingent in the crowd chanted the name of the player whose injury had resulted in his sitting the game out - Willie Cooper - and the loyal defender was persuaded to come on to the turf to join in the celebrations with his teammates. In the days before non-playing squad members received winner's medals, Aberdeen were afterwards given permission by the SFA to strike a special one for a very special servant to the club!

The euphoria of that first ever Scottish Cup success soon gave way to reality, however, as the Dons found themselves struggling in season 1947-48, eventually having to content themselves with a disappointing tenth position in the league. Hibs gained revenge for their Hampden defeat of the previous season when they dumped the Dons out of the competition in the second round. A good run in the League Cup kept the early part of the season alive, although that came to an unexpected end with a semi-final reversal at the hands of lowly East Fife.

The following campaign was even more depressing, with thirteenth position in the table seeing Aberdeen narrowly escape the drop, an opening-round exit at the hands of Third Lanark in the Scottish Cup and failure to progress beyond the sectional stage of the League Cup.

By the early stages of the 1949-50 season, several of the cup heroes had moved on to pastures new, including Willie McCall, Willie Cooper, George Taylor, George Johnstone, Frank Dunlop, Stan Williams and Joe McLaughlin. George Hamilton had also been transferred to Hearts but had returned north after a few months. Among the youngsters beginning to make their mark around this time were Chris Anderson, Archie Glen, Kenny Thomson and Harry Yorston.

On the field, things had improved to what could best be described as 'mediocre', with eighth place in the league, a fourth-round defeat in the Scottish Cup and elimination from the League Cup again at the sectional stage.

Fred Martin

The major changes which Dave Halliday had brought about within the playing staff began to start paying dividends the following season, by which time Fred Martin was the first choice between the sticks, Dave Shaw had arrived from Hibs and Alec Young had signed from Blantyre Vics. The Dons progressed through their League Cup section, only to be foiled by Hibs in a marathon quarter-final tie which was extended to four games before being decided. Both teams had won their home tie 4-1 in the two-leg affair, the first replay had ended 1-apiece (no extra time at this point!), before, as is so often the case in football, Hibs routed the Dons 5-1 in the second replay.

A three-goal, fourth-round defeat at the hands of Celtic ended the Scottish Cup run, whilst in the league, the Dons were right up there challenging until a lapse of form in the second half of the season saw them eventually having to settle for fifth position.

Aberdeen's fortunes took another nosedive the following season and 1952-53 looked to be faring no better, with a poor start to both the league and League

Cup. However, a battling Scottish Cup run, which included replay wins in every round bar the opening, saw the Pittodrie team reach the third final in their history, where they would face the might of Rangers.

Harry Yorston

The team for the final read:- Martin, Mitchell, Shaw, Harris, Young, Allister, Rodger, Yorston, Buckley, Hamilton, Hather. With 135,000 supporters looking on, Harry Yorston salvaged a 'second bite of the cherry' for Aberdeen, with a late equaliser after John Prentice had put the 'Light Blues' in the driving seat. Alas, Harry's goal in the end proved to be superfluous, with Billy Simpson grabbing the only counter in the replay.

One of the most amazing results in the history of the Pittodrie club occurred during the following season. It came in the semi final of the Scottish Cup, when, on 10th April, 1954 at Hampden, the Dons humbled Rangers by six goals to nil to reach yet another Scottish Cup Final. Tall forward, Joe O'Neil, by no means a top-team regular, was the hero of the day with a 'hat-trick', a feat made even more remarkable by the fact that he had sustained a depressed fracture of the skull in a match three weeks previously. The other marksmen on that great day were Graham Leggat, Jack Allister from the penalty spot and Paddy Buckley.

Sadly, the fairytale was not completed and a fortnight later, Celtic lifted the trophy with a 2-1 win, a repeat of the scoreline when the teams had met at the same stage of the event seventeen years before. Paddy Buckley notched the Aberdeen consolation, with the Dons lining up as follows:- Martin, Mitchell, Caldwell, Allister, Young, Glen, Leggat, Hamilton, Buckley, Clunie, Hather.

Aberdeen had also made a bright opening to the league campaign and, although they ended up in ninth place, victory in the final match against Hibs would have meant third position. The barren period in the League Cup continued with another quick exit.

Twice in succession the Dons had been forced to endure the pain of falling at the final hurdle in the Scottish Cup but in 1954-55, they at last lifted more silverware, this time, by securing their first League Championship trophy.

Initial signs that term were not too promising with the, by now almost expected, failure to reach the knock-out stages of the League Cup. Once the league was underway though, it was a different story, with Aberdeen enjoying a superb campaign, which saw them, on the third last Saturday of the season, needing to beat Clyde at Shawfield to win the title. That they duly did, courtesy of an Archie Glen penalty, with the team that day reading:- Martin, Mitchell, Caldwell, O'Neil, Young, Glen, Leggat, Yorston, Buckley, Wishart, Hather. These eleven plus the others who played that season - Allister, Hamilton, Smith, Morrison, Wallace, Brown, Paterson and Clunie - were responsible for ensuring that, after fifty-two years in existence, the Dons had finally been crowned Scottish League Champions!

Having been in charge of Aberdeen since prior to the outbreak of World War II and now led the club to the ultimate achievement of the day, Dave Halliday decided the time was ripe for a fresh challenge and moved on to fill the vacant position at Leicester City in the close season. Into the breach stepped Davie Shaw, who had become trainer at the club when Bob McDermid sadly passed away.

Although the public face at Pittodrie was very positive at this time, there were problems behind the scenes caused, certainly in part, because the players had not received an extra penny from the club in recognition of their achievement in lifting the title. That did not exactly do wonders for the morale in the dressing room and matters weren't helped when Hibernian were elected to be the first Scottish representatives in the newly created European club competition. The reason? The Dons may have won the league but, after all, it was the Easter Road chairman,

Harry Swan, who had been behind Scotland's participation!

Despite the negatives, Davie Shaw did not have long to wait before lifting his first trophy as manager, namely the 1955-56 League Cup. Hibs, Dunfermline and Clyde had been dispatched at the sectional stage, with Hearts and Rangers following in the quarter and semi final respectively. The Dons' Hampden opponents in the 22nd October final were St Mirren.

For the record, Aberdeen's team that day read:- Martin, Mitchell, Caldwell, Wilson, Clunie, Glen, Leggat, Yorston, Buckley, Wishart, Hather, with the 2-1 win coming courtesy of an own-goal and Graham Leggat. Whilst at the time, many thought this would be the start of a glorious run for the new boss, the game turned out to be the highlight of his four-year reign.

Runners-up in the league that season, surrendering their title to Rangers, the Dons also fell at the first hurdle in their Scottish Cup quest, going down 2-1 'away' to Rangers. The following year saw early exits in both cup competitions and a drop to sixth in the table. The slide continued through the following three seasons, with finishes in the league of twelfth, thirteenth and fifteenth and mediocre showings in cup events, other than the Scottish Cup of 1958-59, when the team reached Hampden once again, with the Paisley 'Buddies' again standing between the Dons and more glory!

The Aberdeen side which trotted out on to the Hampden turf on 25th April, 1959 was:- Martin, Caldwell, Hogg, Brownlee, Clunie, Glen, Ewen, Davidson, Baird, Wishart, Hather. Unfortunately, a bad injury to Dave Caldwell in the opening minutes meant Aberdeen were forced to play most of the match with just ten men (it would be another seven years before substitutes were to be permitted in Scotland!) and it was to prove too much of a handicap. Goals from Bryceland, Miller and Baker gave 'Saints' a three goal advantage before Hugh Baird fired a consolation for the Pittodrie team.

In mid-November 1959, with floodlights having been installed at Pittodrie just a few weeks previously, Davie Shaw reverted to being trainer with another ex-player, wizard of the wing, Tommy Pearson, installed as the new boss. As already recorded above, there was no instant cure to the Dons' troubles, however, with escaping relegation heralded as almost being an achievement in itself.

On the playing side, the influence of Tommy Pearson was fairly immediate, with the careers of stalwarts such as Jack Hather and Jim Clunie nearing their end and injuries causing the curtain to fall prematurely on life at the top for Archie Glen and Fred Martin. Pearson encouraged youth to have its fling and the likes of Dave Bennett, Charlie Cooke and Doug Coutts started to make their presence felt.

It would be fair to say that the gamble did not quite pay off and Tommy Pearson became the latest in a long line of fine footballers for whom the transition to management did not produce the desired rewards. Season 1960-61 saw a slightly better finish of sixth in the league which was followed by twelfth (1961-62), sixth (1962-63), ninth (1963-64) and twelfth (1964-65). During this spell, the Aberdeen cup form was nothing short of disastrous, with no Scottish Cup runs to speak of and a total failure to progress beyond the sectional stages of the League Cup.

Jack Hather

The final straw came in the early part of 1965, when, within the space of three games, the Dons were thrashed 8-0 by Celtic in the league, held at home by second division East Fife in the opening round of the Scottish Cup and then beaten by the same opposition in the replay. On 13th February, Tommy Pearson understandably decided enough was enough and tendered his resignation.

A fortnight later, the Dons announced Pearson's successor, a man who, it would be fair to say, laid the foundations for an upturn in the fortunes of the club to a level which, at the time of his appointment, could never have been dreamt by even the most ardent member of the 'Red Army'! That man was Eddie Turnbull.

THE SIXTIES SWING...
ENTER EDDIE TURNBULL

WHILST THE Eddie Turnbull era at Pittodrie began with an encouraging 2-0 'home' victory over Rangers, in which Ernie Winchester and Don Kerrigan were the men on target, the main objective that term was quite simply to stay up. Turnbull, a member of the Hibs 'Famous Five' of the fifties, achieved that, finishing twelfth, and used the remaining months to assess the talent available to him.

Actions speak louder than words and the fact that no fewer than seventeen players received free transfers at the end of the season speaks volumes regarding what the new manager's conclusions were! Very much the 'hands-on' boss, Turnbull overhauled the club's scouting system and brought in new players such as the experienced Harry Melrose from Dunfermline and goalkeeper Bobby Clark from the club Turnbull had left to join the Dons, Queen's Park.

There was an improvement in the league standing in 1965-66, with the side achieving eighth place, and whilst the League Cup witnessed the almost traditional exit in the sections, a good Scottish Cup run was only halted when Rangers squeezed through 2-1 in a Hampden semi final replay following a scoreless draw in the first game.

Things got even better the next season, with fourth position attained in the league and the semi-final reached in the League Cup. Additionally, a superb Scottish Cup campaign saw Dundee, St Johnstone, Hibs and Dundee United all accounted for and the Dons through to another Hampden final against the soon-to-be-crowned Kings of Europe, the mighty Celtic.

For that clash, on 29th April, 1967, the Dons fielded:- Clark, Whyte, Shewan, Munro, McMillan, Petersen, Wilson, Smith, Storrie, Melrose, Johnston. Sadly for the Dons, Celtic were unstoppable at this time and strikes either side of the interval, from Bobby Lennox and Willie Wallace, saw the trophy remain in Glasgow.

At the conclusion of that season, Aberdeen crossed the Atlantic to play in a close season tournament for which, along with other invited sides including Hibs, Stoke City and Wolves, they temporarily changed identity, becoming the 'Washington Whips' for the duration of the event.

The 'Whips' enjoyed a good tournament, winning the Eastern Section to reach the final, where they met Wolves, narrowly losing 6-5 following two periods of extra time. Unfortunately, it was Pittodrie defender, Ally Shewan, who put through his own net to gift the decider to the men from Molineux.

The tournament was excellent preparation for the Dons' first foray into European football, the runners-up spot in the Scottish Cup having gained them entry into the European Cup Winners' Cup due to Celtic having qualified for the European Cup, both as holders of the trophy and League Champions.

A 14-1 aggregate success against KR Reykjavik in the preliminary round was then followed by a narrow 3-2 defeat at the hands of the Belgian club, Standard Liege.

Aberdeen performed reasonably well in the league, finishing fifth to enable qualification for the Inter-Cities Fairs Cup, but did not enjoy much success in the cups, with a second round Scottish Cup exit, courtesy of Dunfermline and a failure to get beyond a very strong League Cup group which included both halves of the 'Old Firm'.

If that season's form was indifferent, the next year was positively mediocre, with league survival becoming the number one priority from early on. When the dust had settled, Aberdeen were lying in a depressing fifteenth place in the table and the European foray in the Fairs Cup had ended with a second-round defeat by Real Zaragoza, following victory over Slavia Sofia in the opening stage. The faint prospect of another European foray in the next season was blitzed by a 6-1 thumping by Rangers in the semi-final of the Scottish Cup and when two of the team's hottest prospects, Jimmy Smith and Tommy Craig, were allowed to move to Newcastle United and Sheffield Wednesday respectively, the alarm bells were starting to ring among the Pittodrie 'faithful'.

Despite prophesies of doom from many quarters, the season actually didn't get off to a bad start at all, with Dunfermline Athletic, Clyde and Hibs dispatched at the sectional stage of the

the sixties swing . . . enter Eddie Turnbull.

League Cup. Unfortunately, further progress was halted by Celtic, who ran out 2-1 aggregate winners in the quarter finals.

Joe Harper

In October 1969, a young forward called Joe Harper, who had impressed Eddie Turnbull when playing for Morton against the Dons, was persuaded to make the move north for a modest £40,000 transfer fee. 'Wee Joe' did not take too long to settle and played a major part in helping the Dons finish in eighth place in the league table, contributing six goals.

The Scottish Cup campaign that season saw doubles from Harper and Davie Robb account for Clyde in the opening round. That was followed by a surprisingly tough 2-1 victory over Clydebank in a match which saw exciting young prospect, Martin Buchan, skipper the side for the first time ever. Jim Forrest and Robb fired the goals that night.

It was a Dons side severely hit by injuries which travelled to face Falkirk in the last eight of the competition. Included in the line-up was young winger, Derek McKay, who had arrived on a free transfer from Dundee earlier in the season and the reserve made the most of his inclusion by scoring the game's only goal to set up a semi-final clash with Kilmarnock.

Retaining his place for the tie at Muirton Park, the inclusion of McKay again paid handsome dividends, as he repeated his feats of the previous round by again grabbing the game's only counter.

A crowd of 108,464 packed into Hampden Park on 11th April, 1970 to witness the fourth final meeting with Celtic in the history of the competition. Having lost out in the three previous occasions, the omens were against an Aberdeen side which read:- Clark, Boel, Murray (G), Hermiston, McMillan, Buchan (M), McKay, Robb, Forrest, Harper, Graham. Sub:- Buchan (G).

The breakthrough came in the 27th minute, when Aberdeen were awarded a hotly disputed penalty after a McKay cross struck Bobby Murdoch on the arm. After lengthy protests from the men in hoops, Joe Harper stepped up to coolly slot the ball past Evan Williams in the Celtic goal.

It stayed that way until seven minutes from time, when that man McKay pounced after Williams had parried Jim Forrest's shot to put the 'Reds' two up. The drama was by no means over though and with less than two minutes remaining, Bobby Lennox reduced the deficit. As Celtic pushed for the equaliser, Joe Harper sent McKay clear and the winger completed the fairytale by placing an unstoppable shot past the despairing Williams. The Scottish Cup, with Martin Buchan, at twenty-one, the youngest player ever to skipper a winning side, had returned to Pittodrie for the second time!

The tale of Derek 'Cup-tie' McKay really was the stuff of dream. The matchwinner of the quarter-final, semi-final and final hardly played again for the Pittodrie side and indeed, never scored for the Dons other than in those three momentous games. However, the Banff-born forward, who was transferred to Barrow in September 1971, will be forever remembered in Pittodrie folklore as the man who brought the Scottish Cup back north after an absence of twenty-three years.

The euphoria which followed the cup success did not take long to dissipate with failure, not for the first time, to reach the knock-out stages of the 1970-71 League Cup, in which Airdrie and St. Johnstone provided the opposition. Hopes of European Cup Winners' Cup glory were soon extinguished, with Honved of Hungary having the unwelcome distinction of being the first team to eliminate Aberdeen from European competition on penalty kicks, Jim Forrest being the unlucky Don who failed with his attempt.

In the league, despite a couple of indifferent early results, things were looking very good indeed, with fifteen wins on the trot between October and January, including a record breaking twelve consecutive shut-outs for Bobby Clark.

All good things come to an end and on 16th January, 1971 Hibs edged the Dons 2-1 at Easter Road. That seemed to signal a temporary change of fortunes, which was not confined to matters on the pitch, as, on the 6th February, much of the Main Stand was destroyed by fire. Part of the history of *Aberdeen Football Club* died that night, as many irreplaceable records and artefacts were lost.

Hopes of retaining the Scottish Cup evaporated in early March at the hands of Rangers, that coming after wins against Elgin City and Dundee United, although, if anything, the defeat proved to be a blessing in disguise, as the Dons renewed their league challenge, which had faltered in the previous few weeks.

Matters came to a head on 17th April, when Celtic travelled north for what was, in all reality, the league decider, with the home side needing both of the points on offer. An early Harry Hood strike saw the visitors get off to a dream start and although former Ranger, Alec Willoughby, levelled matters before the break, the Dons could not break down a Celtic rearguard in which captain, Billy McNeill, was immense. The Parkhead club held out for the draw and went on to clinch the title, whilst the Dons were left to rue the points thrown away when they had gone off the boil in the early part of the year.

Disappointment at having come so near and yet so far was still fresh in the minds of everyone associated with the Dons when, during the close season, the players and fans received another body blow. Eddie Turnbull had been offered, and had accepted, the manager's post at his first love, Hibs. An era, which many argue set the wheels in motion for the success which was to follow, had ended!

THE CALM BEFORE THE STORM

TURNBULL'S departure signified the end of an era, one in which the Club had experienced more than a modicum of success. Turnbull's successor was his right-hand man at Pittodrie, Jimmy Bonthrone. Bonthrone, who worked closely with his predecessor, had taken the opportunity to learn his craft. Now, with Bonthrone in charge, the confrontational days of Turnbull would become nothing more than folklore.

Indeed, Bonthrone could not have wished for a better start to his first season in charge, with the Dons defeating Celtic in the final of the Drybrough Cup pre-season tournament. As usual, the League Cup was the first campaign of that 1971/72 season and hopes were high but unfortunately, a possible quarter-final meeting between the Dons and Hibs was thwarted at Brockville, thanks to a double from a certain Alex Ferguson.

Undeterred, the club made a blistering start in the league and led the table going into November. A seemingly unbreakable grip at the top slackened when Hearts came to Aberdeen. Pittodrie had turned into a veritable fortress, with no club having won there for twenty months but a Donald Ford 'hat-trick' for the ten-man 'Jambos' (two goals in the last four minutes) was enough to give the men from Tynecastle a 3-2 win. The Dons' misery was further compounded when Celtic went top of the table.

 Again, Aberdeen responded in the best possible manner, going undefeated for two months, any opposition being annihilated by a barrage of goals. However, just as with the previous year, February turned out to be a disaster for everyone connected with *Aberdeen Football Club,* when one of the greatest talents ever to grace Pittodrie left for pastures new. Martin Buchan's departure was highlighted when Eddie Turnbull's Hibs knocked a shell-shocked Dons team out of the Scottish Cup and with Buchan gone, only three victories were mustered in the final nine games. The one redeeming feature of the season was the goalscoring exploits of Joe Harper, who netted 33 times, a post-war record. However, English scouts had been keeping an eye out for 'King Joey'..........

Pittodrie was also experiencing a crisis behind the scenes. Turnbull had gone, as had

Drew Jarvie

Buchan and with talk of big-money offers from England, testing times lay ahead. The acrimony which surrounded *Aberdeen Football Club* overshadowed the arrival of Drew Jarvie from Airdrie. All began well for the Dons in season 1972/73, with the team scoring an incredible 36 goals in 5 League Cup games. The Dons were drawn against Celtic in the semi final, a match which proved to be Joe Harper's swansong. Harper smashed the club transfer record when he signed for Everton for £185,000. To make matters worse, goalkeeper, Bobby Clark, was being linked with a transfer to Stoke City, although the proposed move fell through.

Dons fans were in uproar. They had seen their star striker and star defender leave for pastures new south of the border and many vowed never to set foot in Pittodrie again. The Dons fans' fears were calmed though, when Zoltan Varga joined the club from Hertha Berlin. The Hungarian stayed with Aberdeen for just six months but in that time, managed to convince the Pittodrie 'faithful' that they were witnessing perhaps the most gifted player ever to don a red shirt. However, not even Varga could help swell the tide of indifference which surrounded the club's form. To say the Dons were inconsistent would be a gross understatement. The team had scored 8, 7, 6, 5 (twice) and 4 (five times), a feat which makes impressive reading. Unfortunately, they had also drew a blank on no fewer than twelve occasions! The season proved to be one where the Dons fell to Celtic in all three competitions. The semi-final defeat in the League Cup was compounded by defeat at Pittodrie in a fourth-round Scottish Cup replay. Jock Stein's men had also completed a league double and the Dons finished the season in fourth place, 14 points behind the eight-times Champions. The final game of the season was at

Picture Gallery

Billy Dodds

Craig Hignett

David Rowson

Eoin Jess

Inglis and Teddy

Derek Whyte, Jim Leighton & Craig Hignett

Mike Newell

Paul Bernard

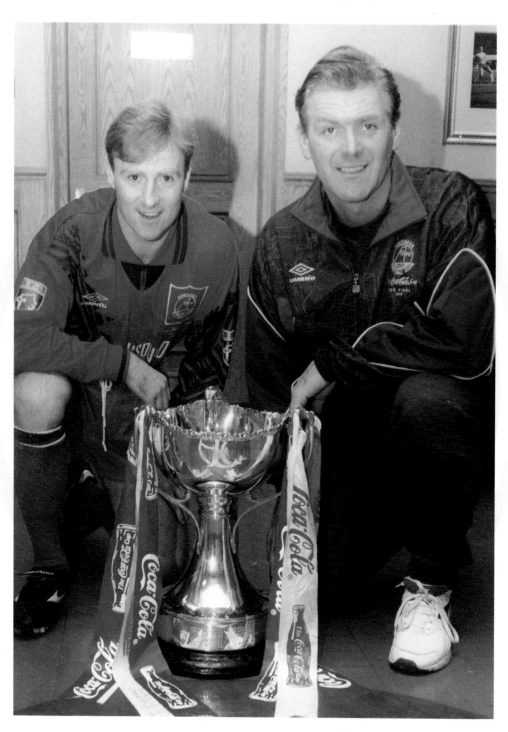

Stewart McKimmie & Roy Aitken with the Coca Cola Cup.

Duncan Shearer

Joe Miller feels the strain.

Alex McLeish jostles with Mark Hateley

Duncan Shearer & Alex McLeish

Alex McLeish in plaster battles on.

Scott Booth

Willie Miller

Cooper puts the squad through a gruelling session.

Dean Windass and Billy Dodds

Eoin Jess skilfully avoids Richard Gough.

Billy Stark

Mark McGhee

Alex Ferguson with the European Cup Winners' Cup.

The many arms of Jim Leighton.

Hans Gilhaus

Alex Ferguson with some of his backroom staff.

Alex Miller

Some old favourites travel to Egypt.

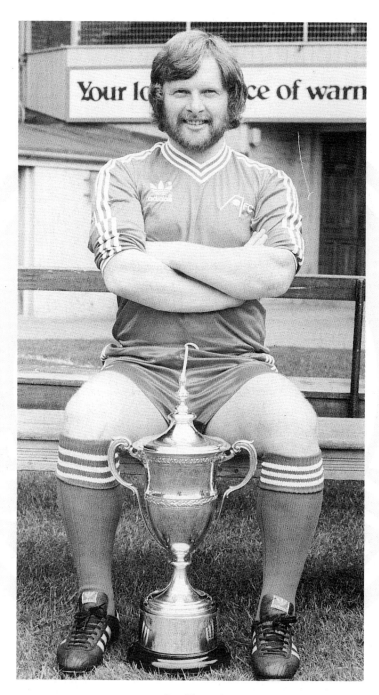

Joe Harper

Steve Archibald

A hard days training.

Ferguson Donald & Anderson.

Alec Willoughby signs autographs.

Eric Black

Cappielow, and Jimmy Bonthrone gave a young defender a run-out in the last half hour. His name was Willie Miller.

Season 1973-74 began with Scottish football allowing two substitutes for the first time ever and it was a season which was to end with Aberdeen being known as draw specialists. The midfield had been decimated over the summer, with Varga leaving to join Dutch masters, Ajax, as a replacement for Johan Cryuff. Captain, Steve Murray added insult to injury when he joined Celtic, whilst Jim Forrest headed out to South Africa. Bonthrone was powerless to prevent the exodus and the pressure was telling on the Dons boss, particularly with former boss, Turnbull, having worked a miracle of sorts at Easter Road. The 'Hibees' were a shambles when Turnbull took over. Now they had won the League Cup and finished higher in the league than the Dons.

A shining star for the Dons was Drew Jarvie, who had proved versatile in attack and in the heart of the midfield. The player had topped the Dons' scoring charts in his first season with the club and would do so again in his second, bringing his total tally to over fifty.

The League Cup quarter final was a case of 'deja-vu' for the Pittodrie team as they were once again paired with Celtic. Drew Jarvie scored twice but the Celts scored three times, and that, coupled with a scoreless draw at Pittodrie, meant the Dons were out. In effect, the season was over by January and Bonthrone was by now walking a managerial tightrope.

The new season was to be the final one of the old First Division. The league was to be restructured and a new Premier Division formed. This meant eight teams would be relegated from the First Division and competition would be intense. Everyone connected with the club felt wary of the season ahead, especially after the previous one; and with Alec Willoughby now gone and Dave Robb missing for almost the entire season, the outlook was far from inspiring.

The Dons failed to qualify from the group stage of the League Cup and with no European competition either, the focus was firmly on the league. The first league game at Pittodrie was against Hibernian, who had a new and familiar face in their line-up. Joe Harper had struggled at Everton and would have jumped at the chance to return to the 'Granite City'. However, it was 'King Joey's' former manager who acted quickly. Harper's return to Pittodrie was not a pleasant one for the Dons fans. A free-kick late on by 'King Joey' levelled matters and Hibs scored a dramatic winner in injury time to hand Aberdeen their first opening day 'home' defeat for fourteen years.

Things did improve and by the end of October the Dons were third, although Celtic once again dented their hopes, winning by a single goal at Parkhead, a result which heralded a run of nine games without a win, before Aberdeen then got back on the winning trail at, of all places, Easter Road. The 'Dandies' were drawn against Champions, Rangers in the third round of the Scottish Cup and it proved to be the highlight of the season. A Miller chip over Kennedy earned the Dons a replay at Ibrox, where the home side were red-hot favourites. A Duncan Davidson header in extra time gave the Dons a 2-1 victory over the 'Light Blues' but unfortunately there would be little else to cheer about for the remainder of the season. The Dons made it through to the quarter finals but a Bobby Graham goal for Motherwell signalled the end of the season. The seventies were proving to be a mirror image of the fifties and a relegation battle lay ahead.....

The beginning of the 1975-76 season saw changes at *Aberdeen Football Club*. Messrs Clark and Robb, the only two of the squad to have won caps for Scotland, welcomed another 'dark blue' Don in the shape of Willie Miller who was fast becoming a favourite with the Pittodrie faithful. Stalwart, Jim Hermiston, retired and striker, Jocky Scott, arrived, unaware at that time that this was the beginning of a sixteen-year relationship with the club. The fans waited with eager anticipation, no more trips to Arbroath or Clyde. Instead, Rangers and Celtic four times a season in the league (the latter six times, following the League Cup draw!). Who would have known that familiarity would breed such contempt?

The Dons made an incredibly poor start to the season, losing 'home' and 'away' to Celtic and Hearts as well as going down 3-2 to Dundee at Dens Park, the last time Dundee would beat

Aberdeen on home territory for many a year. Motherwell denied the Dons their first win at Pittodrie and then came the infamous Dundee United game. Aberdeen were trailing 1-0 to the visitors at half time and shortly after, Joe Smith was sent off for an incident with Paul Hegarty, now, of course, assistant manager at the Pittodrie club. Bonthrone took off skipper, Willie Young, and replaced him with Billy Pirie. The flame-haired 'stopper' became involved in a heated argument with the manager before throwing his shirt at him and storming out. This incredible display was not unusual for Young. He had earned a reputation as being hot-headed and was banned whilst on international duty after he was caught fighting in Copenhagen. The centre-half, despite his undoubted talent, never won a full international cap.

Within days he had joined Tottenham Hotspur for £100,000 and ironically, left the club just a month ahead of Bonthrone. League form did not improve and come October, he was the first Scottish Premier manager to fall prey to the pressures. The Pittodrie board took almost a full month to appoint his successor, with great debate over whether the new man in charge should come from within the club or be an outsider. Aberdeen chose the latter option, overlooking coach George Murray in favour of Ayr United's manager for the past nine years, Ally MacLeod.

MacLeod was never short of a few words and was a very animated character. His time at Pittodrie was destined to be a memorable one and his first game in charge was a 3-0 defeat against Motherwell, following which the new manager's response was the shape of things to come. MacLeod urged Dons fans to come to Pittodrie, *"to see the rejuvenated Dons."* This proved to be poor judgement on the manager's behalf as the match was deplorable. Things became worse, with his former Somerset Park team beating his new charges. Drastic action was needed and it came in the form of Willie Miller, who was appointed captain. Rangers were defeated at Pittodrie and Celtic were overcome at Parkhead. Suddenly, there was hope, so much so that a nine-game unbeaten run saw the Dons in the top half of the table, challenging for a place in Europe.

Ally MacLeod

Just as the 'Old Firm' proved to be the catalyst for a Dons revival, they were instrumental in their swift decline. Rangers defeated the 'Dandies' two Saturdays in a row, in the league and the Scottish Cup, whilst Celtic recorded their fourth win against their rivals that season. The downward trend spiralled into March, when the Dons lost five games in a row. With two games remaining in the league, Aberdeen were fifth, one of five teams battling to avoid the drop, whilst opponents, St Johnstone, were already relegated. The men from Perth had not won in 28 games and incredibly, had not kept a clean sheet since the opening game of the season. A victory for Aberdeen would have ensured their Premier survival but, incredibly, they went down 2-0. Hibernian were the visitors on the final day of the season and the home team knew it was a 'must win' scenario. Aberdeen were awarded a penalty early on but Robb had his spot-kick saved. As the tension grew, Jarvie scored on the half-hour mark with a crisp volley. Joe Smith doubled the lead before Robb, a mainstay in the side for 10 years, snatched the third. Results had favoured the Dons and they were safe.

With the great escape now complete, manager MacLeod sent for reinforcements for 1976/77. 'King Joey' had returned to Pittodrie at the end of the relegation battle but the signing deadline had passed and Harper was ineligible. Now twenty-eight, the 'King' still had 100 goals in him. Stuart Kennedy also joined the new regime, as did Dom Sullivan. The Dons cruised through to the last eight of the League Cup, with Harper scoring in all six games. A replay win over Stirling Albion saw the 'Reds' move into the semi finals, where they were paired with Champions, Rangers. This was to prove the highlight of MacLeod's tenure as

Aberdeen boss. The rampant Dons crushed the Champions 5-1 in one of the biggest shocks of the decade and, safely through to the final, Celtic awaited.

The Dons went into the final sitting proudly at the top of the League but Celtic were overwhelming favourites, owing to the fact that this was their thirteenth consecutive appearance in the League Cup Final. However, the Dons stood proud and goals from Jarvie and Robb ensured the 'Granite City' would have its night. The line-up for that match, on 6th November, 1976, was:- Clark, Kennedy, Williamson, Smith, Garner, Miller, Sullivan, Scott, Harper, Jarvie (Robb), Graham. With the new rule change, the Dons were admitted entry into the UEFA Cup and MacLeod was seemingly a Messiah. However, the second half of the season proved to be a let-down, with only five wins in nineteen games, ensuring the Dons would finish third. The Scottish Cup campaign also ended quickly, with Gordon Strachan's Dundee putting the Dons out. Aberdeen were so bad that day that match-rigging allegations surfaced. Naturally, they turned out to be nonsense but the Dons did finish the season on a high, having rediscovered their self-belief. Off the field, Willie Ormond quit as national boss and the telephone at Pittodrie began ringing....

With MacLeod off to look after the national squad, Aberdeen would have to search for another manager. There were three candidates for the job, Alex Stuart, Alex Ferguson and Billy McNeill. Stuart had done a fine job as MacLeod's successor at Ayr but they were not prepared to lose another manager to the Dons. Alex Ferguson had just guided St Mirren to the First Division Championship but was still inexperienced. McNeill was also inexperienced as a manager but had learned his trade under the legendary Jock Stein - a quality which swung the decision his way. As with previous seasons, the Dons always seemed to lose a fans' favourite in July. This time round it was Arthur Graham, who joined Leeds United, but his replacement, John McMaster, proved to be, if anything, even better. The 1977-78 season was to prove to be one of great excitement for all Dons fans.

McNeill's debut was against Rangers in the league opener at Pittodrie. Goals from Harper and Jarvie gave the Dons a 3-1 win and Dons fans were full of hope. Eleven points from a possible twelve, RWD Molenbeek in the UEFA Cup and Rangers in the third round of the League Cup signified the good times were coming back.

However, two defeats in the league later and out of Europe, the Dons' interest switched to the first leg tie at Ibrox in the League Cup. Aberdeen had not conceded more than one goal a game to Scottish opposition but the 'Light Blues' hammered six past the 'Dandies'. It took until December for the Dons to recover and by then they were fourth in the league, with a lot of ground to be made up. During the slump, McNeill lost one player and acquired a new one. Joe Smith was forced to retire through injury and a young Gordon Strachan came to Aberdeen from Dundee.

Steve Archibald

In January 1978, another two new faces came to Pittodrie in the shape of Alex McLeish and Steve Archibald. The Dons went undefeated in the league for the remainder of the season and marched into the final of the Scottish Cup with no problems. The final game at Pittodrie proved to be an ironic one, as Alex Ferguson's St Mirren went two goals up in the first ten minutes before eventually being pinned back and defeated 4-2. The Dons, who had fought back in the title race, were a point behind Rangers going into the last game of the season but they could only manage a draw at Easter Road whilst the 'Light Blues' defeated Motherwell. McNeill had a week to recharge the batteries of his players for one final effort against the new Champions in the Scottish Cup Final. The Dons put up a resilient effort in the Cup Final but were beaten 2-1. Jock Wallace had led the 'Gers to another 'treble' but it was McNeill who was voted 'Manager of the Year'. Another blow was set to hit the Pittodrie club, though, as Jock Stein stepped down as Celtic's manager and there was no doubt who his replacement would be.

Once again Aberdeen were left with nobody at the helm but the wait for a replacement would be a short one. Alex Ferguson had been sacked by St Mirren and the Dons wasted no time in signing up the young Glaswegian, who had built up quite a reputation as a hot-head. The Aberdeen fans were very quiet on Fergie's appointment, as they knew very little about the man. They would certainly know a lot more by the time he left. Dave Robb left to go to America, with Ian Gibson and Ian Fleming also leaving the club. Bobby Clark broke a knuckle in pre-season and a young 'goalie' named Jim Leighton was thrown into the deep end.

Jim Leighton

Aberdeen made a good start to the season, with a scoring draw at Ibrox and a 4-1 win over McNeill's Celtic. However, as the weeks wore on, points became harder to come by and there were rumours of players being unhappy with their new boss. In fact, the Dons went three months before they won another game and by mid-March they had slumped to mid-table. In a season where the title race was wide open, the 'Reds' could only finish fourth, failing to capitalise on their opponents' poor form.

The domestic cups provided comfort for the fans, as the Dons enjoyed good runs in both. In the League Cup, Rangers ran out winners, 2-1 and Hibernian knocked the 'Dandies' out in the semi final of the Scottish Cup. Ferguson had survived his first season in charge, whilst Joe Harper continued to rewrite the scoring books, netting 33 that season. What followed in the 1979-80 season would prove to be the beginning of something quite special. Dom Sullivan joined Celtic, with Dougie Bell joining from St Mirren. Bell and the fringe players were to make a huge impact on events over the course of the season.

The opener at Partick Thistle was a nightmare, with the Dons going down to a last-minute penalty, courtesy of a McLeish handball and Ferguson's now famous remark, *"Don't laugh, but I've got a scent about the way things are going to turn out this season."* A first-round defeat in the UEFA Cup at the hands of Eintracht proved to be a blessing in disguise for the Dons. The Pittodrie side defeated Rangers 'home' and 'away' in the third round of the newly sponored Bell's League Çup. Celtic followed suit in the quarter finals and Morton were disposed of in the semi to earn Ferguson's men another bite at a cup final winners' medal. The final against Dundee United was a drab affair and finished goalless. The replay at Dens Park was a nightmare for the team from the 'Granite City', as they went down 3-0 in atrocious conditions, handing Jim McLean's side their first trophy.

As with the previous season, Aberdeen were mid-table with games in hand. Twenty points from eighteen games was hardly encouraging and fans were beginning to wonder whether another barren season was on the horizon. They would get their answer soon enough. Celtic and Rangers were in a period of transition and Aberdeen needed to start winning if they were to challenge for the title. The Dons won twice at Parkhead in the space of 19 days, their third win at Parkhead during the season. Rangers had been beaten five times, if only they had the prize to signal their arrival as a competitive force. The title went to the last day, with the Dons trailing Celtic by a point. Celtic need to win at Love Street to be sure and the Dons needed a win at Easter Road. Win at Easter Road they did, ramming five past debutant, Dave Huggins. At Love Street, Celtic were awarded a penalty ten minutes from time. Incredibly, the referee consulted his linesman, changed his mind and the Saints held on for a draw. Aberdeen were Champions, the first outwith the 'Old Firm' for 15 years. The Dons drew 1-1 at Firhill to consolidate their position and the extensive celebrations began!

The summer was a period of great change for Aberdeen. Steve Archibald joined 'Spurs' for £800,000 and Joe Harper also left. Harper, now 32, had struggled with injury and was not able to 'graft' as Ferguson wanted 'his' team to do. His replacement came in the form of Mark McGhee, a bargain at £70,000 from Newcastle. With Dundee United having taken the League Cup, Scottish football was about to be dominated by the 'New Firm'. The 1980-81 season began with the Dons losing Bobby Clark to injury and Jim Leighton was called in to replace the veteran. Nevertheless, the 'Dandies' made a great start to the season, sitting 3 points clear of Rangers and 6 ahead of Celtic. The European Cup proved to be a lesson for the club, as Liverpool won 5-0 on aggregate. The men from Anfield went on to lift the trophy. Aberdeen on the other hand, were stunned.

McMaster had been badly 'crocked' by Ray Kennedy in the Liverpool defeat and doubts were raised as to whether he would ever be the same again. A few weeks later, Gordon Strachan suffered a stomach injury against Dundee, one he would take months to recover from. With half of the season remaining, the Dons had lost their midfield and effectively, lost the title. In the Scottish Cup Morton knocked the Dons out, Andy Ritchie scoring the only goal. The only highpoint for the Dons was Mark McGhee, who was voted 'Players' Player of the Year', the first Don to be so.

Season 1981-82 began with one new arrival, Peter Weir. Weir would prove to be a very important part of Ferguson's jigsaw. Fergie wanted Weir so badly, he offered £200,000 *plus* Ian Scanlon. Emerging through the youth ranks were two raw young strikers, Eric Black and John Hewitt, two players who would become part of Aberdeen's history. Dundee United ended the Dons' League Cup campaign but the UEFA Cup campaign was alive and well. That is, until Hamburg came. The Dons were leading 3-1, Strachan having missed a penalty. With the team counting the seconds, Rougvie fell in a heap; but the Dons kept playing instead of kicking the ball out and Hamburg broke up the park and scored. Ferguson was incensed with his players and rightfully so. In the second leg, Hamburg scored and the Dons were out. Come January, the Scottish Cup was all the Dons had left and they were determined to win it. Their cup form seemed to rub off in the league and Ferguson's men put together a superb run, winning 15 out of 16 games. Incredibly, the Dons were only a point behind Celtic heading into the final game of the season. The scenario this time was that the Dons needed to beat Rangers by 5 or more and Celtic needed to lose. The Dons won 4-0 but Celtic won, too, which left the Scottish Cup as Aberdeen's only chance of silverware. The Hampden hoodoo was finally ended, as the 'Reds' crushed Rangers 4-1 in the Final to earn themselves a place in the European Cup Winners' Cup. The season which followed was arguably the greatest in the history of the club.

GLORY OF GOTHENBURG AND THE TEAM OF THE DECADE

THE EARLY part of season 1982-83 gave no indication whatsoever as to what lay ahead, with defeat in the League Cup at the hands of rivals Dundee United, albeit at the quarter-final stage, following progression through the section, where Morton, Dundee and Dumbarton provided the opposition.

August also saw the commencement of the European Cup Winners' Cup campaign, with the Dons giving themselves a tremendous confidence boost with an 11-1 aggregate hammering of Sion of Switzerland in the preliminary round.

Paired with the Pittodrie side in the first round proper were the little known Albanian outfit, Dinamo Tirana, who displayed more than competent defensive qualities when they left Scotland after the opening leg, trailing only to a single John Hewitt strike. However, the second leg saw the boots quite literally on the other feet and this time it was the men in red who showed how to frustrate the opposition. The match ended scoreless and Aberdeen were through to the second round.

The Dons' league form at this time was anything to write home about, with September's points total amounting to three, courtesy of a win over Morton and a share of the spoils at St. Mirren. The other two matches had ended in reversals, 'away' to Dundee United and at home to Rangers.

Back on the Euro trail, Polish side, Lech Poznan, stood between the Dons and a first ever appearance in the last eight of a European competition. Again the first leg, which took place on the 20th October, was at home and following a nervy opening forty-five minutes, strikes after the break, from Mark McGhee and Peter Weir, gave Aberdeen a two-goal cushion for the return a fortnight later.

Any worries regarding the second leg proved to be unfounded and a Dougie Bell goal, with almost an hour on the clock, saw the Dons safely through to the mouthwatering prospect of a quarter-final meeting with the mighty Bayern Munich. The fact that there was a four month gap before the next game was more than sufficient to keep the 'Red Army' going over the long winter period.

Success in Europe had begun to pay dividends on the domestic front and after that indifferent start, the Dons began to move swiftly up the table, with Celtic once again the main threat.

The defence of the Scottish Cup had also begun in bright fashion, as Hibs and Dundee were dispatched 4-1 (Weir, Simpson, Watson and McGhee) and 1-0 (Simpson) respectively. A visit to Firhill was the Reds' reward for reaching the quarter finals but before that there was the small matter of the trip to Germany to face a Bayern side which was going into the tie as overwhelming favourites.

On 2nd March, 1983, four days after defeating Celtic to go top of the league table, Aberdeen, superbly led by Willie Miller at the back, produced one of the best defensive performances ever by a Scottish club away from home in Europe. Against some of the biggest names in the sport at the time, such as Augenthaler, Breitner, Hoeness and Rummenigge, the visitors were unlucky not to snatch a breakaway goal to win the clash. However, nobody in the Dons' party was anything other than happy with a goalless draw to take back to Pittodrie.

A 2-1 success at Partick Thistle to reach the last four of the Scottish Cup gave Aberdeen the ideal boost just four days before the second leg and on 16th March, twenty four thousand souls packed into Pittodrie Stadium for what was to prove to be one of the most memorable night's in the Club's history.

After only ten minutes, things looked bleak, as the aforementioned Augenthaler broke the deadlock with an absolutely fearsome drive from all of thirty yards which Jim Leighton in the 'home' goal did very well to even get a hand to. However, with half time looming, Neil Simpson scrambled the equaliser to send the Dons in at the break with at least a fighting chance of going through.

Come the 61st minute, though, that hope looked to be completely misplaced. A superb volley from Pfugler restored the Germans' advantage and with less than half-an-hour to go and the Dons needing to score twice to survive, the brave run looked to be coming to an end.

With a quarter of an hour to go, Alex Ferguson sent on John Hewitt in place of scorer, Simpson and within sixty seconds, the Dons were again on level terms. The famous 'mix-up' free-kick routine between John McMaster and Gordon Strachan worked a treat and Alex McLeish was on hand to nod the ball past 'keeper, Muller.

If the home fans were in raptures at that, they went into overdrive a minute later, when substitute Hewitt knocked the ball beyond Muller after the 'goalie' had saved well from Eric Black. Astonishingly, Aberdeen had twice come from behind to score three times against one of Europe's top sides and reach the semi final of the Cup Winners' Cup.

Unfortunately, reversals at the hands of Dundee United and St. Mirren saw the Dons title hopes falter in the period leading up to their Euro 'semi' meeting with Waterschei of Belgium. All that was put on the back burner on the 2nd April, when, in another unforgettable Pittodrie Euro experience, two goals inside the first four minutes, from Eric Black and Neil Simpson, effectively ended the clash with the Belgians as a contest. The Waterschei spirit was well and truly broken and, with further counters from Mark McGhee (2) and Peter Weir, Aberdeen went into the second leg with an unbelievable 5-1 advantage. Two weeks later, nobody was really bothered that the Dons lost a low key return leg by a single goal. The almost unthinkable had become reality. Aberdeen were in the final of the European Cup Winners' Cup with only the small matter of Real Madrid standing between Willie Miller's men and the coveted trophy itself!

Whilst the Pittodrie team's chances of winning the league title had receded somewhat, there was still every possibility that Alex Ferguson and Co would successfully retain the Scottish Cup. A Peter Weir goal against Celtic at Hampden in between the two legs of the Waterschei games had set up a repeat of the previous season's final, with Rangers desperate to avenge their extra-time disappointment. However, that one was not until ten days after the Cup

Winners Cup' meeting with Real, which was to take place at the Ullevi Stadium in Gothenburg.

Every one of the fourteen thousand or so Dons fans who was present in that Swedish stadium on the night of 11th May, 1983 has their own memories, their own feast of stories from what was destined to be the greatest night in the history of the Club. Before the match, not for the first time in that particular campaign, the Dons had been dismissed as 'also rans' against a Spanish team which had been crowned European Champions on no fewer than six occasions. However, any team which can give Bayern Munich a goal of a start twice in one game and still come out on top cannot be taken lightly!

In conditions more akin to autumn in the North-East, with the rain pouring down non-stop, Aberdeen got themselves off to a start which not even their most ardent of fans could have dreamt of. After seeing his volley come crashing back off the crossbar in only three minutes, Eric Black put the 'Reds' in front in the sixth minute after good work from Alex McLeish following a corner. All of a sudden the pre-match predictions did not look quite so accurate!

Seven minutes later, though, it was one-apiece. Alex McLeish's intended pass back to Jim Leighton was intercepted by Santillana, leaving the Dons' number one with no option but to bring the Spanish forward down. The resultant spot kick was gratefully converted by Juanito.

From then on, though, it was the men in red who looked the far more likely to score, with Gordon Strachan, Eric Black and Neale Cooper all coming very close to adding to the Aberdeen tally. However, when the ninety-minute mark arrived, there had been no further scoring and the game went into extra time, for which John Hewitt replaced the limping Eric Black.

With eight minutes to go and the Spanish team happy to settle for a 'penalty shoot-out', Peter Weir broke down the left, something he had been doing very successfully throughout the game. After ghosting past a couple of defenders, he sent Mark McGhee clear and the striker's left-foot cross, which was just out of the reach of 'keeper, Augustin, was met by the onrushing Hewitt, who secured a place in the history books by heading the ball home.

The Dons still had a few nervy spells to endure, notably Salguero's free-kick, which Italian

Willie Miller

referee, Menajali, ordered to be retaken. The defence held firm, though, and scenes of unrestrained joy greeted the final whistle. *Aberdeen Football Club* were Champions in Europe and it seemed as though every inhabitant of the 'Granite City' turned out the following day to welcome their heroes back. Few fans will need reminding that the team that night read:- Leighton, Rougvie, McMaster, Cooper, McLeish, Miller, Strachan, Simpson, McGhee, Black (Hewitt), Weir.

As if lifting a European trophy was not sufficient, ten days later the club retained the Scottish Cup, with Eric Black scoring the only goal of the game against Rangers at Hampden.

The 1983-84 season began reasonably well and by October, the Dons were top of the league. That prompted interest in boss Alex Ferguson from Rangers, until the Ibrox club were told by the Aberdeen supremo that he was not available under any circumstances. Fergie then emphasised the point by signing a new five-year contract. By the beginning of November, Akranes and Beveren had been dispatched in the Cup Winners' Cup, ensuring the Dons' participation until at least the following March, when the quarter final against Ujpest Dozsa of Hungary would take place.

On 20th December, nobody could argue Aberdeen's right to call themselves 'Kings of Europe', when they defeated Hamburg 2-0 at Pittodrie to lift the European Super Cup, the result following a scoreless first leg in Germany the previous month. The win was made all the sweeter by the fact that the Germans had eliminated the Dons from the UEFA Cup in 1981.

When the Hungarians won 2-0 in the first leg of the Cup Winners' Cup quarter final,

Aberdeen looked to be heading out of Europe and when Celtic sent the Dons crashing out of the League Cup a mere three days later, the season looked as though it was falling to pieces, although the fact that the league and Scottish Cup 'double' was still 'on' is indicative of how high the expectation was at this stage of the club's development.

However, in yet another of those unforgettable European nights, a goal from Mark McGhee, his second of the night, with just two minutes of normal time left, sent the

Alex McLeish

return leg against Ujpest into extra time. The additional period was only three minutes old when McGhee completed his 'hat-trick' to ensure the Dons' progress into the last four.

A narrow win over Dundee United, with Mark McGhee again the man who mattered, saw the Dons squeeze into the last four of the Scottish Cup after a replay, where they would meet Dundee. Kilmarnock and Clyde had been Aberdeen's earlier victims.

In early April, Aberdeen returned from Portugal trailing by a single goal to opponents, Porto, after a gutsy performance in the opening leg of their Cup Winners' Cup semi final. They then reached the domestic Cup Final for the third year on the trot, Ian Porteous and Gordon Strachan ending Dundee's chances at Tynecastle.

Hopes of a second consecutive Cup Winners' Cup Final appearance ended on a misty April evening at Pittodrie, when the Portuguese, some years later to be accused of bribing the referee, doubled their advantage over the Dons with a strike from Vermelinho. Such was the performance of the visitors that night that they really did not need to bribe anyone to achieve the desired outcome.

The league title was confirmed as returning to the North-East on 2nd May with a single goal victory over Hearts at Tynecastle, the decisive effort coming from young defender, Stewart McKimmie, ironically his first in senior football. The Dons would be competing in the European Cup the following season.

Prior to that there was still the matter of becoming only the third side, after Queen's Park and Rangers, to win the Scottish Cup three years in a row. That they duly did, with a 2-1 extra-time win over Celtic (Eric Black and Mark McGhee), in which Parkhead skipper, Roy Aitken, who would become the Dons' manager just over a decade later, was sent off for a first-half foul on McGhee. With the 'double' under their belt, Aberdeen were, by quite a way, the best team in Scotland.

The close season witnessed the departure of key players, Gordon Strachan, Mark McGhee and Doug Rougvie, with Frank McDougall and Tommy McQueen arriving. The new-look side took a while to gel and was shocked by Airdrie, then managed by former Pittodrie boss Ally MacLeod, in the League cup.

The European Cup campaign ended at the first hurdle, with defeat in a 'penalty shoot-out' at the hands of Dynamo Berlin. The opening leg, in Scotland, had been won 2-1 by the Dons, with an Eric Black brace doing the trick. In Germany it was an identical scoreline, with Ian Angus on target in that one. The subsequent 'shoot-out' saw Willie Miller and Eric Black's efforts saved, with Ian Porteous, Tommy McQueen, John Hewitt and Billy Stark all scoring.

Following victories against Alloa Athletic, Raith Rovers and Hearts, Dundee United spoiled the Dons' plans for an unprecedented fourth consecutive Scottish Cup success, when they won 2-1 at Tynecastle in the semi-final replay, after the first meeting had ended scoreless. Ian Angus was the Aberdeen scorer.

In the league though, the Dons had led for most of the campaign and on 27th April, when Celtic made the trip north, Alex Ferguson's men required a point to retain the title in front of their own fans. Although Roy Aitken gave the 'Hoops' the interval advantage with a penalty, it

Alex Ferguson

was fitting that skipper, Willie Miller, was the one to head home what proved to be the decisive equaliser. Aberdeen had retained the Scottish League title for the first (and to date, only!) time in their history!

The success continued into 1985-86, a season which was to prove to be Alex Ferguson's last one in charge. By October, the Skol Cup was already in the trophy cabinet, following a remarkable run which witnessed Ayr United, St Johnstone, Hearts, Dundee United and finally, Hibs all dispatched without a single goal being conceded. An Eric Black brace and Billy Stark did the damage in the final.

By this time, the Dons boss was doubling up as Scotland manager after the tragic death of Jock Stein and it was a dual role he seemed to be perfectly capable of fulfilling, although after the Skol Cup win, Aberdeen's league form, particularly away from home, took an alarming dip, killing off any possibility of a third title in succession.

By Christmas, though, Aberdeen had secured their place in the last eight of the European Cup, thanks to wins over old foes, Akranes and Swiss outfit, Servette. Gothenburg awaited in the quarter final and an emotional return to the Ullevi Stadium was eagerly anticipated.

Once again, the Dons seemed to be reserving their best performances for the domestic cup competitions and by the time the 'home' leg of the European tie against the Swedes arrived, wins against Montrose and Arbroath had seen Aberdeen safely through the quarter final, where they had been drawn to meet Dundee.

Gothenburg, winners of the UEFA Cup four years previously, proved to be no mugs and left Pittodrie with a 2-2 share of the spoils to keep the tie very much alive. Willie Miller, playing in his fiftieth European match, and John Hewitt grabbed the 'home' goals.

Dundee also proved to be no pushovers and after a 2-2 draw at Dens Park, in which Hewitt scored both, the Dons required extra time at Pittodrie before Peter Weir notched a brilliant winner with a chip over 'keeper, Bobby Geddes. Earlier, Eric Black had equalised after Ray Stephen had given the men from Tayside a shock lead.

Seven days after that win, the Dons travelled to the scene of their greatest night ever. However, it was destined not to be a happy return and in a disappointing match, neither side managed to break the deadlock. Aberdeen were out of Europe on the 'away goals' rule.

With the Dons now out of contention in the league (they were to finish fourth), the Scottish Cup was their sole chance of adding to the Skol Cup already won. The Pittodrie side, who had never lifted both domestic cups in the same season, breezed into the final in a repeat of the previous October's League Cup win, with another three-goal victory against Hibs. Again Black and Stark both found the net, with Joe Miller the other marksman.

Standing between Aberdeen and glory were a Hearts team still trying to come to terms with the fact that Celtic had pipped them for the league title by the narrowest of margins. After just five minutes, it was apparent that the 'Jambos' were heading for the role of bridesmaids yet again, when John Hewitt put the Dons in front. Second-half goals followed from Hewitt and Billy Stark and to complete a miserable afternoon for the maroons, skipper, Walter Kidd, was red-carded for throwing the ball at Neale Cooper.

Although the close season witnessed the departure of Eric Black, Neale Cooper and Frank McDougall, the 1986-87 term started brightly enough, with midfielder, Billy Stark, underlining, his goalscoring ability with six during August alone. September began badly, though, with Celtic winning a Pittodrie' 'penalty shoot-out' 4-2 to reach the semi-final of the Skol Cup. For the record, John Hewitt and Willie Miller were the unlucky Dons to miss from the spot.

In the Cup Winners' Cup, the Dons had been paired with Sion, the team they had thrashed four seasons previously. In the first leg in Scotland, the men in red had to come from behind to take a narrow 2-1 advantage to Switzerland, Jim Bett and Paul Wright the scorers. The return leg proved to be a total disaster for Aberdeen, with the Swiss taking the lead after just four minutes and going on to score twice more. To make matters worse, Jim Bett was dismissed for his second bookable offence with more than half of the match remaining.

That early exit from Europe certainly did not help in the Club's bid to hold on to their prize asset – boss Alex Ferguson – and in November, the hammer blow fell with the announcement that he was off to Manchester United to replace Ron Atkinson. As if that wasn't bad enough, the news that his assistant Archie Knox, the natural successor to Ferguson, was going as well, left the board of directors with the task of looking for an external replacement.

Speculation was rife as to who the board would appoint and it's fair to say the man charged with the responsibility of following in the footsteps of the Pittodrie club's greatest ever manager was not on any of the 'possibles' lists. To say that the arrival of former Sunderland player, Ian Porterfield, was a surprise, is one of the understatements of the century!

Porterfield's career at Aberdeen started well enough, although the Scottish Cup campaign floundered at the first hurdle, with defeat by Celtic, albeit it took the Parkhead men three games to dispose of their opponents.

The season ended with Aberdeen in fourth position in the league and Porterfield telling the 'Red Army' that the next season, his first full one in charge, would be the one to judge him on.

Sadly, 1987-88, after a bright opening spell in which the team went on a sixteen-game unbeaten run, turned out to be something of a disaster, which resulted in the departure of the manager at its conclusion, along with his assistant, Jimmy Mullen.

On the field, yet another 'penalty shoot-out' loss saw Rangers snatch the Skol Cup after a six-goal Hampden thriller. Feyenoord had knocked the Dons out of the UEFA Cup at the second-round stage, Dundee United had reached the Scottish Cup Final at Aberdeen's expense and fourth position had been achieved for the third year in a row in the Premier League.

Of the players brought in by Porterfield, the biggest name by a long way was former Celtic star, Charlie Nicholas, from Arsenal. Unfortunately his arrival at the start of 1988 coincided with the downturn in results which signalled the end for the management team.

Porterfield's replacement was the then coach at Pittodrie, Alex Smith, who had been recruited by his predecessor from St. Mirren. Also brought on board were former Pittodrie stars, Jocky Scott and Drew Jarvie, from Dundee, as co-manager and assistant manager respectively.

Again there was an early European exit to suffer, this time at the hand of Dynamo Dresden in the opening round of the UEFA Cup. The Skol Cup followed the same pattern as twelve months before, only this time round Rangers took the match in normal time with a 3-2 victory.

Dundee United also followed the pattern of the previous season by knocking Aberdeen out of the Scottish Cup, although this time it was at the 4th-round stage, with United going through thanks to a late Mixu Paatelainen drive in the second replay.

In the league, with Charlie Nicholas showing exactly what he was capable of, the Dons pushed Rangers all the way, finishing in the runners-up spot and enjoying the satisfaction of spoiling the Ibrox team's celebrations with a 3-0 'away' win on the final day of the season.

Going into 1989-90, the Dons fans were beginning to get somewhat restless, having had to endure a barren three seasons. Another opening round Euro exit, against Rapid Vienna in the UEFA Cup, did not help matters. However, in October, the Dons at last lifted their first trophy with Alex Smith at the helm.

Skol Cup wins over Albion Rovers, Airdrie, St Mirren and Celtic meant that, for the third year running, it was to be a Dons - Rangers final. This time, though, it was the men from the North-east who came out on top, two goals from Englishman Paul Mason, a purchase from Gronigen, doing the damage in a 2-1 win after extra time.

By this time, Smith had used connections in Holland to purchase Mason, Theo Snelders as a replacement for Jim Leighton and 'striker', Willem Van der Ark. And in November, Hans Gillhaus, at £650,000 the Dons' record signing, arrived from PSV Eindhoven, enjoying a sensational debut at Dunfermline, in which he scored a first-half double in a 3-0 victory.

Again, though, it was Rangers who took the title, with Aberdeen in the runners-up position. However, there was still time for another trophy to make a welcome return to the

'Granite City', this time in the shape of the Scottish Cup.

Partick Thistle, Morton, Hearts and Dundee United were Aberdeen's victims en route to a final meeting with Celtic at Hampden on 12th May, 1990. History was made, in that, with one-hundred-and-twenty minutes of football failing to produce a goal, it became the first Scottish Cup to be decided by a 'penalty shoot-out'.

Also, from a Dons perspective, further history was made, in that it was to be the first occasion when, after four failed attempts, the Dons would actually come out on top in a game to be determined in such a manner.

The 'shoot-out' scoreline was an incredible 9-8 for Aberdeen, with defender, Brian Irvine, firing the decider. The Dons had entered the nineties in much the same way as they had spent a lot of the eighties, with two cups in the trophy cabinet!

THE 'NEARLY MEN' OF THE NINETIES

1990-91 will forever be remembered as the season when for many fans, the Dons blew the title by getting their tactics wrong in the final game of the season. However, to put everything down to the game with Rangers on 11th May (the very *date* should surely have ensured success for the men from the North-East!) is surely being somewhat simplistic.

After a comfortable start to the season, with Skol Cup successes over Queen's Park, Stranraer and Hearts, Rangers prevented the Dons from reaching the final of the competition with a narrow win in which Trevor Steven grabbed the only goal.

Three days later, on 26th September, 1990, there came the incredible scoreline from McDiarmid Park......St. Johnstone 5 Aberdeen 0! Not only that but David Robertson was sent off in the first half and there were rumours of infighting within the Dons camp. A few days later some semblance of order was restored when Salamania of Cyprus were beaten 3-0 at Pittodrie in the return leg of the opening round of the Cup Winners' Cup, following a 2-0 success away from home a fortnight previously.

There were further problems for the Dons on the following Saturday, when Theo Snelders suffered a fractured cheekbone, courtesy of a challenge from Ally McCoist, in a goalless draw at Pittodrie played in atrocious conditions. Snelders would miss much of the season and with Michael Watt lacking experience in the top flight, Alex Smith brought in Andy Dibble on loan.

The Englishman was ineligible for Europe, although Watt was certainly not at fault as the Dons exited at the hands of the experienced Polish side, Legia Warsaw.

With the focus now firmly on the league campaign, the Dons embarked on an impressive run which took them to the top of the table and by the end of the year, with young Eoin Jess, in particular, looking the part, Aberdeen were right up there challenging with Rangers at the top of the table.

January, though, brought the Dons back down to earth with a bump. Defeats from Dundee United and Celtic left the Pittodrie side seven points adrift of Rangers, whilst in the Scottish Cup, Motherwell had the temerity to come to Pittodrie and win, thanks to a stunner from substitute, Steve Kirk.

Whilst at that point Rangers appeared to already have one hand on the Championship, the mid-season decision to scrap relegation and revert to a twelve team set up had a positive effect on the Dons. The pressure was off sides previously under the threat of the drop and Aberdeen slowly, but surely, began to close the gap on their rivals.

On the penultimate Saturday of the season, Motherwell shocked the Ibrox team 3-0 at Fir Park on the same day that the Dons were beating St Johnstone. The upshot was that the pair were going into the last game of the season level on points and 'goal difference'; but with the Dons having scored two more than their Glasgow opponents, a draw would be sufficient to see the league trophy return to the North-East.

Perhaps the lack of necessity to win worked against the visitors, as Alex Smith opted for a more defensive formation than had been implemented throughout the season. Peter van de Ven replaced fellow Dutchman, Willem van der Ark and injury ruled out Brian Irvine and Theo Snelders, with Michael Watt deputising.

A hefty Mark Hateley challenge on young Watt inside the opening minute set the tone for the afternoon, the Dons' 'keeper requiring quite a bit of treatment. Jim Bett and van de Ven both scorned opportunities, the latter's, in particular, a gilt-edged chance, before, with the interval looming, Hateley broke the deadlock with a header. Ten minutes after the break, the Englishman added a second and to all intents it was 'game over'. Scott Booth and van der Ark were both introduced into the fray but to no avail - Rangers had won the game and with it, the League Championship.

In the immediate post-Fergie era, any manager at *Aberdeen Football Club,* as Ian Porterfield had already found out to his cost, would find the burden of attempting to live up to what had gone before, almost unbearable. By 1991-92, the situation was not much different for Alex Smith and a season without a trophy was perceived as failure by the fans, irrespective of the fact the team had come so close to lifting the league.

A quartet of victories at the start of the season offered, what proved to be, false hope and for the first time for many seasons, Aberdeen lost three on the trot on 'home soil', two of the games in cup competition.

Firstly, Airdrie, newly promoted from the First Division, knocked the 'Dandies' out of the Skol Cup, courtesy of a John Watson counter. Next came St Johnstone for a league visit and despite going a goal behind and having Davies sent off before the interval, the men from Perth rallied to record a 2-1 win. If that caused a mood of unrest within the supporters, following the 1-0 'home' defeat by Danish side BK1903 Copenhagen, there was *rebellion* in the air, with a sizeable number staying behind to vent their wrath at the manager.

Inevitably, the Dons were dumped out of Europe, the Danes winning 2-0 on 'home' ground, and the miserable run in the league continued, coupled with defeat at the first hurdle of the Scottish Cup by Rangers. A home defeat in February proved to be the last straw, resulting in Alex Smith earning the dubious distinction of becoming the first Aberdeen manager to be officially sacked.

As to who would take over the helm of the listing ship, one name stood out head and shoulders above the rest as far as who the *fans* wanted to be in charge. Injury had forced Willie Miller to hang up his boots earlier than he would have wanted, although he had been retained in a coaching capacity by the club. The fans got their wish and the greatest defender ever to have graced the red shirt was duly appointed, taking charge for the first time in a goalless draw with Rangers on 25th February.

By the time Miller took over, he was too late to prevent Aberdeen from ending the season in sixth position, their lowest for fifteen years and one which meant no European football the following season. Things could surely only get better?

The new boss had already purchased Mixu Paatelainen from 'New Firm' rivals, Dundee United, shortly after his appointment and in the close season, surprised many by persuading former Celtic skipper, Roy Aitken, to join as player / assistant manager. Also coming in was

Fort William–born striker, Duncan Shearer, and in September 1992, Blackburn Rovers' battling midfielder, Lee Richardson.

The campaign proved to be a case of 'so near and yet so far', with a Dons side led by 28-goal Shearer, ending up in the runners-up position in the league, the Tennents Scottish Cup and the Skol Cup.

Rangers, largely due to an amazing unbeaten run of thirty three games, including cup-ties, deservedly took the league title, with the Dons again having to make do with the silver-medal position, although unlike two seasons previously, the destination of the Championship was apparent long before the last game.

Willie Miller's first final in his new role was the Skol Cup in October, with the mighty Rangers, the opponents. Hamilton, Dundee United, Clydebank and Hibs had all been dismissed on the road to Hampden.

An adventurous 4-3-3 formation, which had been successfully deployed in the league, saw the Dons take the game to their opponents. However, the 'Light Blues' took the lead when Stewart McCall took advantage of Theo Snelders indecision as to whether a ball which had come off defender, David Winnie, would be classed as a pass back under the newly introduced ruling. The Dutchman, in attempting to chest the ball down, allowed the midfielder in to prod it home.

On the hour mark, with Scott Booth having just been brought into the action, Aberdeen were level, when Duncan Shearer shot home from Winnie's cross. That signalled extra time, during which defender, Gary Smith, had the misfortune to head past his own 'keeper and give Gers what turned out to be the winner.

It was the same opposition who faced the Dons the following May in the Scottish Cup Final, an encounter which was switched to Parkhead due to redevelopment at Hampden. Frustratingly for Willie Miller's side, the outcome was identical to the other cup final. Neil Murray's opener was deflected past Snelders by Brian Irvine and just before the break, Mark Hateley added the decisive second. Lee Richardson reduced the deficit with less than a quarter of an hour to go but by then it was a case of 'too little, too late' and Rangers held on to win the match and with it, the domestic 'treble'.

The following season marked the opening of the new Richard Donald Stand and the Dons celebrated by going through the month of August unbeaten, although the first day of September saw Rangers end their chances of further progress in the League Cup with a 2-1 win in extra time, the Dons' cause not helped by the loss of a first minute penalty.

Aberdeen bounced back by stringing together a run of results which put them top of the table come the end of September. By that time they had also clinched their Cup Winners' Cup second-round berth with a comfortable 7-0 aggregate success against Valur of Iceland.

In the second round, Italians, Torino, would obviously prove to be a somewhat sterner test. The opening leg was in Turin and for the first half-an-hour, the Dons put on a display equal to anything ever witnessed previously. By that time, goals from Paatelainen and Jess had given Aberdeen what should have been an unassailable advantage. However, Sergio's strike on the stroke of the interval gave the Italians hope and, buoyed by the goal, further counters, courtesy of Fortunato and Alguilera, turned the tie completely around.

Despite losing what should have been an unbeatable lead, Aberdeen were by no means out of the tie and Lee Richardson's early opener at Pittodrie gave the 'Red Army' real hope. Alas, that hope was misplaced and goals either side of half time, from Carbone and Silenzi, were sufficient to give the men from Turin a 5-3 aggregate win.

The Dons' early promise in the league was not capitalised upon and yet again Rangers took the Championship, with Aberdeen once more in that second spot.

Disappointment was also the order of the day in the Tennents Scottish Cup, with a last four dismissal by eventual winners, Dundee United, after defeats against East Stirling, Raith Rovers and St. Johnstone.

For all the wrong reasons, season 1994-95 will go down in the history books as one of the most memorable for the Pittodrie club. As well as the implementation of three points for a league victory, there was also the introduction of 'play-offs', with the second-bottom side in the Premier League facing the First Division runners-up in a two-leg affair.

It was also a campaign for which the Dons prepared with several experienced players having moved on. Lee Richardson had returned south, Mixu Paatelainen had been transferred to Bolton, Jim Bett was playing in Iceland, Robert Connor was at Kilmarnock and Alex McLeish was the new boss at Motherwell. Brought in by Miller as replacements were Billy Dodds, John Inglis, Colin Woodthorpe and Peter Hetherston.

The season got off to a disastrous start with defeat at the hands of Latvian minnows, Skonto Riga, undeniably the worst result ever in the Dons European forays. That humiliation had an alarming effect on the confidence of the squad and by late October, a horrendous run in the league left the Pittodrie team just one place off the bottom.

A reasonable run in the Coca-Cola Cup, with Stranraer, Partick Thistle and Falkirk all accounted for, ended when Celtic won in extra time in the semi final at Ibrox.

A brief revival in the league, with a six-game unbeaten streak, did not last and in February, a 3-1 reversal at Kilmarnock had Aberdeen in bottom place. Almost inevitably, that meant the end of the road for Willie Miller and two days later, at an emotional press conference, chairman, Ian Donald, who had taken over from his late father Dick, announced that the club was looking for a new manager.

With time at a premium, the board took the decision to promote Roy Aitken to the position of caretaker manager. The former Celt made a dream start when, in front of the television cameras, Aberdeen recorded a 2-0 victory over Rangers, with goals from Billy Dodds and Duncan Shearer.

Within six days, the Dons' new boss experienced the extremes of the game. If the Rangers game had given the fans renewed hope, the result the following Saturday plunged them into a despair greater than any previously experienced. Stenhousemuir 2 Aberdeen 0 in the fourth round of the Tennents Scottish Cup was, quite simply, one of the blackest days in the club's history.

The defeat by the Second Division club was followed by more poor results and as the season drew to a close, it looked more and more likely that Aberdeen would be relegated for the first time ever.

A Billy Dodds brace in the third-last game gave some hope of a reprieve and when that was followed by a 'home' win over Dundee United, it was the Taysiders who were staring the drop in the face. The atmosphere inside Pittodrie that afternoon was electric and there's no doubt the support played no small part in securing the 2-1 victory, in which Dodds and Duncan Shearer were the marksmen.

A two-goal win at Falkirk completed the league programme with the Dons in ninth place and Dundee United down. To complete the Houdini act, Dunfermline had to be accounted for and they duly were, with the Dons winning both legs of the 'play-off' by a 3-1 margin. Top flight status was maintained but it was an experience nobody associated with the club ever wanted to endure again.

Roy Aitken's position was made permanent prior to the start of the new season, whilst former player, Tommy Craig, joined as his assistant. A solid start was made to the league and in the Coca-Cola Cup, St Mirren, Falkirk and Motherwell were all dispatched before Rangers stood between the Dons and a final appearance.

On a wet evening at Hampden, with Eoin Jess outstanding, a Billy Dodds brace helped Aberdeen to a 2-1 win over their Ibrox rivals. Just a few short months after they looked set for the drop, Aberdeen were in a cup final. On 26th November, 1995, the fairytale was completed when Dundee of the First Division were beaten 2-0 at Hampden, courtesy of counters from Dodds and Shearer. The Dons were winners again - and back in Europe!

A cup 'double' looked 'on' until Hearts took advantage of a below par performance from the Dons in the semi-final at Hampden. A small measure of revenge (in reality, an *extremely* small measure!) was exacted when Aberdeen pipped their Edinburgh rivals for third spot in the league behind the 'Old Firm'.

The first competitive match of season 1996-97 was in the unlikely setting of Lithuania, for the UEFA Cup preliminary round, first-leg, tie with Zalgiris Vilnius. Goals from Dodds (2), Stephen Glass and Duncan Shearer saw the Dons take a healthy 4-1 lead back to Scotland, an advantage they almost squandered when the Lithuanians, who had driven to Aberdeen from London by coach, inflicted a 3-1 defeat against a team which took the field expecting to win by the length of Union Street. Stadium announcer John McRuvie's playing of *'The Great Escape'* on the final whistle hit the nail on the head!

Welsh Champions, Barry Town, were beaten 6-4 on aggregate in the first round proper, before Brondby of Denmark scored late on in each half at Pittodrie to take a two-goal advantage to Copenhagen, where it finished goalless.

The defence of the Coca-Cola Cup ended when Dundee avenged their reversal from the previous November, with a 2-1 quarter final win, whilst interest in the Scottish Cup failed to advance beyond the third round, when Hibs, with none other than Jim Leighton between the sticks, won a Pittodrie 'penalty shoot out' in a replay after a 2-2 draw at Easter Road.

After the drama of twelve months previously, the league campaign was tame by comparison, as, with ten wins and fourteen draws, the Dons ended the season in sixth place.

There was a fair degree of optimism going into the new season. Gary Smith and Eoin Jess had both rejoined following short spells at Rennes and Coventry City repectively, Brian O'Neil arrived from Celtic and Jim Leighton came back to his first senior club to be immediately installed as Captain. The fifth summer signing was ex-Everton and Blackburn Rovers striker Mike Newell, who had been at Birmingham City.

Season 1997-98 began with a scoreless 'home' draw against Kilmarnock. Roy Aitken had freely admitted there were far too many occasions when the Dons were having to settle for a share of the spoils. It had cost a substantial amount of points the previous season and here they were again, back in the old routine!

The following week at Tynecastle, after an excellent opening twenty minutes, in which

Mike Newell put the visitors ahead, Hearts ran out 4-1 victors. As the season continued, the alarm bells started ringing as the Dons form alarmingly mirrored that of two years previously. The knives were out for Roy Aitken and when, in the televised game at Tannadice on 9th November, Aberdeen were humbled 5-0 by Dundee United, his time was up and the following morning he was shown the door along with his assistant, Tommy Craig. Porterfield, Smith, Miller and now, Aitken.........whilst prior to the Fergie era each may have been given more time, new standards had been set at Pittodrie and it was proving difficult to find someone who could live up to them.

Whilst the search for a new boss was being carried out, former 'Spurs' boss, Keith Burkinshaw, who had been recruited as Director of Football, took temporary charge and in his opening game, at home to Rangers, as was the case with Roy Aitken, masterminded a creditable 1-1 draw.

With both Willie Miller and Roy Aitken having cut their management teeth at Pittodrie, the board elected to go for experience this time round and on 21st November, the new man in the 'hot seat' was revealed.......former St. Mirren and Hibs boss, the Coventry City and Scotland assistant manager, Alex Miller.

A NEW BROOM SWEEPS CLEAN...
THE MILLER REVOLUTION

Alex Miller

WHEN Alex Miller took over, one of the first things he did was to publicly state he would keep *Aberdeen Football Club* in the Premier League and he was as good as his word.

By the end of the season, Aberdeen were in sixth position in the table but had suffered an early cup exit, again at the hands of old foes, Dundee United. The one signing Miller had made during the season, though, was a significant one - international defender, Derek Whyte, from Middlesbrough, for a bargain £100,000. Whyte's presence steadied what had been a shaky rearguard and at the beginning of season 1998-99, the former Celtic man was appointed team skipper, with Jim Leighton becoming Club Captain.

At time of writing, the new season, the first in the new Scottish Premier League, is about to get underway. Several players have left, including Brian O'Neil, Dean Windass, Stephen Glass and Bulgarian international, Tzanko Tzvetanov. Others have been brought in . . . Craig Hignett from Middlesbrough, Andy Dow and Stuart McCaffrey from Hibs and Aberdonian, Mark Perry, from Dundee United. Others look set to join and there is a genuinely positive feeling within the club.

Off the field there have been other significant changes, with additional investment brought in to augment the share issue of 1995. Successful businessman, Stewart Milne, is now chairman, with Ian Donald becoming vice-chairman. The next major decision for the Board of Directors, is whether to invest more money in Pittodrie Stadium or, alternatively, to investigate the possibility of re-locating to a 'new green-field' site.

Whilst relocation away from Pittodrie would be a sad event for Dons fans of all ages, at the end of the day, *where* the Dons play is secondary to *how* they play. The spectre of Alex Ferguson appears to have haunted all who have followed in his footsteps. However, in Alex Miller the club would appear, at last, to have found a man who really could bring back the good times the success-starved support has craved. Can he do it? Only time will tell.